SPACE CREATOR[s]

MaxWell Shell

Copyright © 2014, 2021 MaxWell Shell

All rights reserved. No part of this publication
May be reproduced, stored in A retrieval system
or transmitted, in any form or by any means,
electronic, mechanical, photocopying, recording,
or otherwise, without the prior written
permission from the author.

AcknowledgeMints go out to the editors
of publications where some of these PO Ms
Appeared or are forthcoming.

ISBN: 978-0-9856715-6-3
1ˢᵗ Print(s) June 2014
2ⁿᵈ Print(s) September 2021

Printed at 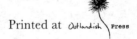 Outlandish Press

For my PeepHoles!!!

Introduction	9
TopOff/ \OffTop	11
Whiskey Kisses (Dizzy Island)	12
Wish Number One	13
Truth Be Told	15
The Never Ending Engine That Runs	17
Gray Traffic	18
Stargasm	19
Had A Dream	20
The Mess Age	22
Internal Pockets	25
Propeller Prompts	26
Quote The Boat(s)	29
"Old Crank Key" (Chapped-errs, circa early-errs)	31
1-5-1	32
in this moment	33
speaking of love	34
untitled sum total	36
Refrigerator Magnets	37
fun da mint tool language	39
in there/out there	40
little lite houses	41
Falling Joy	42
present tints	43
brain froze angles	45
played in the shade	46
how cool hike whose?	47
untitled bank teller	49
Getting Over Dogmas	50
Water Break	51
Beautiful Fool	52
Beautiful Fool Too	52
Women's Ears	53
King Mean	54
He'll show you She's real	55

Quote UnQuote	55
long gone wrong song	56
Lovely Ugly	57
Poets & Politics	58
Typical Literal	59
thirst things thirst	60
say when (uncle bin)	61
trash talks	62
All Purpose Tanka(s)	64
typing time (4)	65
Braille Breath	66
rot bottom	67
hard to beat	68
summer buzzard	70
Hallucination Heart	72
poetic-pathetic	73
I'm Cool (R U?)	74
UpDated UpBeat	75
lonely only	76

MAX/ON\ /MAX\OFF   77

Thee O Pressed	78
Typing time (1)	79
Bubbles	80
cabbage patch (over my eye)	82
words like (an epic epilogue)	85
about my future poetry	88
Spontaneous Angles	89
Haikus Too	90
Words Ain't Massive Enough	92
Free Verse for thee Uni Verse (one)	94
A short one for more won	95
Firm Grip (A No Pen Poem)	96
STAR STUDENT(s)	98
INDIGOLDEN CHILD	99
The children that	101
The Children That Wondered Why	103
A PO M	104

Introduction

Within these pages you'll discover the poetry of MaxWell Shell. And, to be sure, you are in for a treat. MaxWell, unlike many poets of his generation, bridges seamlessly the performative word with the written page. No one, in my 25 years of teaching writing, captures as unique a voice. Yet, much has already been written about today's young Black poet. And, who am I to add to that critique. Yet, what MaxWell offers in these pages transcends review. Within, you will find a distinct absence of cliché metaphor and aphoristic definitions of man's experience with the darkness and reflections that are his life. From epic visionary to ambitious wordsmith, MaxWell makes definitions on his own terms—remaking words with choruses that literally take form and dance upon the page. Simply, his prose is like none other, as he disfigures both syntax and traditional style while, at once uncoupling and rebuilding a whole new life for the words that we've grown overly accustomed to.

To your great benefit, you have purchased his works. So, despair in your endeavor to absorb his meanings and capture the glimpses of his insights— for the close and deliberate reader can revisit his text, time and again, while relishing that each new insight is but a mere shadow of the depth brought on by the author's task. Bathe now in his imagery and pine for his incredulity and irreverent indifference. MaxWell: for a voice and tenor as inimitable will unlikely be seen again in his generation.

Dr. Brad Hammer

TopOff/ \OffTop

Whiskey Kisses (Dizzy Island)
for Astra lala lala

SirRounded
 By WizKid
   Emerald
     Odd OZness…

  PinkFloyds
& PurpleReigns
& WildGalloping
     PictureFrames…

Flicker Flames &
    All Desire
Caught up on the
       Tallest Wire…

Flawless Fire
& FurMinted Sounds
       Bubbling
Up from Noblest Crowns.

Wish Number One

If I had A Photographic Memory
I'd have building designs, blueprints
of curtains & blinds, stored inside
A World-Series of files/I'd mirror each child
                with my Memory's Smile.

I'd be an Architect,
Foreman, A Dark-Erect dwarf in
the Constellation of Conversation—
      my science, my Art,
my political pinch/scorched in/

with intentions to escort them

           to Escalator Skeletons
    to stairwells with swelling limbs
to know any & every machines makeup &
              to put it on for them.

Compute it, commute thru to it:
Beautiful Blue Notes in Music.

I'd make everything from SCRATCH
(food, clothes, shelter)—i'd
    steal what I needed BACK.

I'd fly planes, conduct trains/symphonies,
Learn Languages'til my brain
just burst with Assembly lines of imagery…
[capturing Magnificent Miles of Peach-Tree Scenes]
        as my camera swings like A chimpanzee
    catching banana-cream-pies with my face

              as madder dreams die in its place.

I'd have to take
           My Time
but i'd wait
           for no one
    to read my poems
because i'd be the
                PO M
      that tastes

& feels & smells & sounds

           & is seen
      risking its smile
to
      forget
           its
                mouth.

Truth be told

I've been
    A very
unhealthy writer.

The type to
Type A LuvLetter
To anybody out there
& not care who gets it
Because I never write
    that specific…

If it ever got that vivid
My alphabet letters
Would turn into pictures
    To burn & learn
    How to remember
    What once existed:
        A punished image…

A hundred gimmicks in A row

SuperMarket lines
    & rhyming radios
Running the streets like pantyhose
& Love looking like candy clothes—

Edible & eaten off…
But No pedestal for
    her heat or soft…
Just A pillow for her sleepy toss…
& little pills for her sheepy thoughts…

& she be lost
& he be boss
& these be
Heeby jeebies
Glossed & glazed
& I am not Amazed

[High in A sky box
 it's still A box
Regardless of how high
 The market value was
Around the time you paid]…

Each price
Is A vice
Is A grave
Is A booby trap
    & U R prey.

Truth be told
We can take control
& sway our souls
    Which Way
       ?

(the never ending engine that runs)

the never ending engine
that runs off love & on
    & on it runs

        unbelievably
Achieving heat
& warmth &
      A cool that cools
     the hottest guns
in the most heated palms

& drops love-bombs
  from Parachutes
        to carry Truth
            that shoots Beyond

      & lands in LoveSongs
      SungSymbolically
   on Hate's FrontLawns

& basks in dusk
    until TheSun
      surrenders
        to itself,
     determined to
inspire with fire,
       learning it is
   the never-ending
engine that will
       never run out of Dawns

      (because it never really sets
        & forever HorizonRises:

        an *italic island*
     of **BoldGold Psalms**)

Gray Traffic

to be human is to be

a dogmatic
automatic
ultra sensitive
culture electric
color magnetic
prophetic flower

in some
seductively secure
coat of a habit.

unexpected
but accepted.

headed to who
knows where.

like dreamers.
like forfeiting screamers.

like religion worshippers
& fire starters.

like permanent markers
and sweeter juice.

phenomenal
whenever we let loose
of absolute truths
and proselytizing proofs.

because in that moment
possibility is present.

STARGASM:
for Sabrina

U make an
Extreme Dreamer
Dream Extremer))—

Stellar Streamers on
Astral-Striped Bikes—

Candy Stripes can't hold
A molecular match to your
            Beauty's Witness—

A Jupiter-Infused
Athena-Forgiveness:
An Isis Brightest Bridge
          to Burn Relentless—

Invigorating Invitation
to Envision ImagineNations
within ImagineNations ReInvented—

Eccentric Citric-Scented
Cyclic Electric-Tinted Spectrum
     Circling Purple-Greens/
 Hurdling Perfect Wings Angelic—

& breathless i breathe in this moment:
knowing only Love's Greatest Intention
          has led me to this PO M

((Had A Dream))

1.)
Had A dream About
A fist-fight breaking out
After the quickest of DissAgreeMints:
Unholy Holes in the Holland-Heads of
Hollerin' Males Squabbling like A cock-fight
but more like A cat-fight & I instantly left
the scene. Exiting with
         A head-shaking unease.
Wondering when will boys learn to wake up
from this kind of snore-charged sleep
& recharge their Masculine Batteries
& dream dreams at peace with themselves
as well as their immediate & extended Family
    that need them to take time to breathe.

2.)
had A dream inhibitions were prohibited
like an infant's original initiative
& as they grew they grew into their
busyness & didn't use liquid-dating spirits
or sniff-fable spirits or lung-killing spirits
    to give them this fulfilling
    feeling of clearly remembering
their every experience splendiferous

3.)
Had A Dream
Manipulation
Didn't get Nominated
Or Denominated to be
The Riddler, Crippler
    Or Enabler of
    Hypocrite Nations
Taking Hippocratic Oaths
    With The Cure Tucked Away
In an All-Too Brief Suit-Case Safe
Chicken-Noodle Soup/Behind-Bars///Soap

4.)
had A dream
ABOUT the REVOLUTION
i want to be part of:
where every thing was
medicine music & smart love…

silver screened science
meets green horn-knit innerG
meets trustworthy innovations
& cosmically inclined chemist-trees…

meets baby blooms & young lady wombs
        with young gentle men
    in tune with their infinity
& cape-Ability of loving more than one
like little krypton creatures
      reaching for the sun
& sons & daughters raised Montessori Freely
    with hip hop in their hearts
       & classic-cool music in their minds
& their blood pumping life-spraying graffiti
with bodies that dance to the rhythm of
              IMAGINE-NATION
          PEACE TREATIES

    (had A dream i just
    couldn't stop dreaming)

"THE MESS AGE"

1
Angelic Astronaut Ask me not
      my Assigned Astrology:
  Only Thru Aligned Astronomy
could I Answer that Question Logically…

Alan Freed Expression is All I Need
to seize my Sign's Psychology
& Freudian slip into A mint-tool
slick enough to trip phlegm up &

      corkscrew with Life's Lobotomy…

To Acknowledge Me is to Acknowledge U
& without one rule of thumb i'm numb:
      pressed Against A fecund fence;
branches, Antlers, AmpPool GrassDew runs…

2
Baby Bear's
GoldenLocked
Perfect Fit
Hornet Snot

Honey Dripped
On Pollen Pots
Of Alchemy's
Allergic Plot…

This Grave Situation:
O No It's Not
That Low or Hot
So Cold & Cocked
  Back to Scold
the Whole Damn
Parking Lot

Drive-In Theater

Fear of Sun
SunBlockedFor
Darkness Clearer

3

The Momentum Factor
as its Called or
 will be called
when i call it
will be Called off
like cats & dogs
in the last great reign in August...

All is relative.
All is lawless.

Only Love can
Problem-Solve this...

Whatever this is
that involves All this
Flooding Forward}}}}
 {{{Fire Song-Lit

4

Forfeit
Only Pride & Pulpit,
Politics, Perverted
PretentiousPerplexed
 PreCautious, PedaPhallic
Permanent PreDetermined
Poorness, Poverty,
Prostituting Pimps Puking
PurePromise Per Premise Pressed In;
 if Heaven be Honest...
The Proposal ofAny ProperTease
 Preposterous.

 PostHumorously GhostPolished
 AutoPilot HotPockets

5
Toot Toot
Goes The Horned Horn:
It Shoots thru whale-holes
& the former latter is reborn
    in Another MatterLess Form…

Has SatUrn no Scorn
like A WombMan too warned?

****

Baby Baby
Burn Burn
TranceFormed!!

[INTERNAL POCKETS]

1
"Check The
Genetic Code:
ELECTRIC BOLD"

2
"This Life
holds U liable.
Don't buy the Bull."

3
"Sew your
dreams greater
& S-cape the
Seamless Haters."

4
"From Rabbit Ears
to Magic Riches
EveryWhere."

5
"M-Brace The Sun
& Catch A BearHug
From The Breeze"

6
"Live The Lion.
Fly The Eagle.
Rise & Fall &
Rise Again."

7
"ClevelandCity
UniverseAbility"

Propeller Prompts

(3)
Insatiable Fear!,
Your Sensational
   Persuasiveness
Gives Nations gifts of
Crazy Love running Away
so quick it hits its head
until it sees stars
(illiterate-bred until
   it reads hearts)…

just this much…

A whole-grain start
A no-brain end…
A scared crow's flinch
A pro-pain parched by
A low-drain's dark
& very old men
play with hope-hang cards…

No faith in A March or
    An April that May
flip this desperate deck
  into not feeling this way

(4)
Flashes of Flood-Light
filled her eye-wells up
like Orwellian Gestures:
(("purple passages"
      Jesus of Nazareth
      Cartoon Clouds with
      HeliumBalloon-sized
         AlphaBet Letters))

She swears she knows better
but stays kicking herself with
    LoveLetter Spurs & it
    doesn't occur to her

she must not have served the
            proper higher power
All this time she's spent drenched
            with her own tears
while on this good mother earth…

i smile & it occurs to me she is
not used to kind words followed
            by kinder actions
& knowing this kind of thing happens
All Around this NeverMind World
i remind her it is time for
Opening up like A clam for pearl
& to take her hands off that
            mother-of-pearl
& Allow herself to smile: All pearls…

(7)
out like A lamb's last supper
in A Lion's first Louisiana Summer:

       A Hundred-Hyena Mirage
         laughs uncontrollably
like The Sun petting & stroking heat
upon its favorite spaceship
            patrolling fleece—

grease sweats out of jive-turkeys no longer
                into getting baked
but still wanna get dressed & stuffed—
too much to finish their empty plate.
      Animated Limbs gravitate
toward the skin of their Origin…

A UV cool-scene sugar-laced Tropic-Cool
      Kool-Aid ladled & pouring in
           means more to men than
                  All the Money in this world.
      An Authentic ImagineNation
            is All they wish—

A ProCreation that CoExists with Love
the lamb, the lion, the lips that kiss
       & get kissed
       & !Go Fish!

   only for moments like this—

       Nectar Victorious
  if you get my Gorgeous Drift
       for A BackDraft that Fresh & Crisp
       Briskly breaking thru Cerebellums:
singing songs of Love's long lost MotherShips
      Creating Space for more Magic & Myth

"Quote the Boat(s)"

1

there's A Carnivore
starving for more than
meat to eat… & herbivores
with words like swords
         that swerve onto curbs
    like vehicular spurs
             & eat thru
      tough streets like
        well done beef…

2

U want to be strong like an Ox?
Eat fire & fly like A fox?
    Be the GrandFather Clock
& the fast slobber knocked?
Free from Boredom, Bad Breaks
       & Last Stops?

3

      I bring U glass in A shot.
I sing U grass-dew with gravel on top.
  I pitch the fork & pinch the tint
    to wake up dreams that only squint
((& never get to sleep that deep))…

"Old Crank Key"
(Chapped-errs, circa early-errs)

[1-5-1]

no combination lock or
any known nomination block
where mayors & governors
are born like hustlers

& from president blood
    comes the kings of
        crimes incredible

& their mothers regret
    ever letting them
survive to exit thru

to forever do
    what is
A pathetic fool's
        game:

        playing
    while getting
        played

        childish
        as any
          old
        stingy
        stain

[in this moment]

in this moment
there are more
    mints to come…

less death and
more life to live
    thru two lungs…

in this moment
 my choice is
  my destiny

    &
"regardless" is the
    retarded mantra
      that is also
        my secret recipe…

[speaking of love]

U know,
the kind
that's always
on my mind.

Where he & she
& she & he & we
& we be family...

Extremely
Dreamed
     by me
      for mine.

Pour wine from vineyards
Allow each child its smiles & dinners
               & for breakfast
the full course of all its potentials...

there is A machine in place that men use
& women/children/men get used by

but there are ways to manipulate these
game show machines to make it seem not
               as true by
        buying true lies
           from everyone
        speaking of love...

never knew i
needed love
to be true i
always thought
i could just be cool

  i never knew
i was speaking of love
'til the day
  U dyed
your blue
eyes brown
just to show me
  how much
U was down…

like poetry's
lovely sound.

like magic practiced
from under A crown.

[untitled sum total]

can A lack of confidence be cured
           by dishonesty discouraged?
not sure of the plot per
vessel expressed thru obvious words…

not words but actions
impacted by passion perturbed…
positive reactions (free actions)
                          ((free words))…

& greed serves these errs freely
by being free too freely…
no, by being greed too greedy…

by buying poverty & feeding fodder
to the needy for their foreheads are for beating…
stubborn man want to be ram repeating
                            ram ram repeating…
program deleting
  is what i'm needing…

quicksand & quicksilver
           bleeding

[Refrigerator Magnets]

1
there with eggs & bed
flood me blue he said

2
their purple beauty
      winter rock
    shadow chant
     summer wind

3
    part true
produce two

4
moment sing
      hit sit
weak ship

5
have me gone
less behind?
recall playtime.

6
next fast
rain stare
trip drool
trudge none

7
blood she water
shot chain road
though think
storm petal-ing
     this away no

8
one fly silence
mind told attitude
justice juice cool
      hide hood jive
         slammin' crew

9
enough trash
ego check
pity bold
cheap flash
hard noise
def fame
loud ice
hang high

[fun da mint tool language]

Refresh Mint
Pep per Mint
      Spear Mint

Whatever Mint
We're Meant
to be (fresh)
to be (pep / per)

(spear in) our flesh]
            for fear
            we will
one day see clearly

without mouth to say it:
within skin that sacred.

[in there/out there]

in here
sincere
is impossible.

out there
they cut off air &
equip hospitals.

in here
big fear
is our obstacle.

out there
money's mirrors
reflect thee unstoppable.

in here
pain is baby
& powder blues.

out there
gain is crazy
& there are
countless fools.

in here
learning is
not logical.

out there
what is fair
is what you're
not allowed to do.

in here
is infinite.

i'll be out there
in a minute.

[little lite houses]

sections of sectioned off sequences
succumbing to the frequentness of
the streams they're released in—
like air in A gill/water in A lung;
both of them could kill or be
killed by thee other one…

my brothers from another mother
haven't really thought about where
they're from or how they came to be
      the most unexplainable seed…

my sisters with their
hips flared & lip layered
posing like they don't care
hoping that someone sees them there
      & wants to treat them fare…

our value system is violence
our malnutrition is silence
our mannerisms are animated ammunitions as
we listen to the animals' creep-up of predator
                competitor prices…

we know better than to voice
      our voyeuristic voices
unless it's an Artistic Gesture
      like the sun setting on
                Heaven's Island…
regular
      unleaded
            premium

  an arsonist sun leaving them ignited…

[Falling Joy]

Can U Imagine
A Prettier Picture
Any Clearer or
      More Mirror

For Glorious Theater
that stakes stages
like A Vampire Slayer
on paced pages
of LoveThought
      & WorkArt

& thru her heart
my muse stays
      boosted like
Armies Recruited

but when they march
O they march like
Marvel Carnivals

the music of mutant men
evolution men
      new music men
who begin to win
      by retuning them

because the program been set

but with her still Around
the childs is bound to
find what need to be found

& it's on its way down i bet

[present tints]

English is A gift
because it molecules
monologues & atoms

Attitudes into minuscule
miniature beakers of spite
speaking to science:

NIGHT IS **dark**
& death is *light*

& life is sort of
Love & Loyalty &
Over All Respect for
          Royalty

so check the KINGS
& the things they
    bring…

[peasants
   not
presents]

revolt only
we don't
vote

& can't stamp the stallion
damp & dollars & dog-tired
from what they All call SIRE

& the higher he is
& the more on fire she is
& the war of worlds is boys & girls
& the answer is not Jesus.
& the answer is not Hip Hop.
& the answer is not politics.
& the fact of this matter
it doesn't matter what matters
more or less because all matter
           is bottomless.

& out of this
my power is
A source of
its own blood
   bones &
bouncing risks.

[brain froze angles]

& goals
gone hunting
gathering
    money

& hungry as ever
    the edge of
heads of corpse
    co-operations

& clever
    sports
pre-occupations

& we should all get paid
for sweat blood
    & levels laid
that made A grade
A degrading distraction—

All A's: an Artistic Abstraction

[played in the shade]

never before
by the bed or
the shore
have i heard
such words
from the dead
bread of birds

so instead of her
getting her chance
to dance with wings
she stands back
& plans an attack/
animals stack &
she stabs me

[but i'm not cut
because i got up]

woke straight
from the dream/
broke leg:
every
thing…………………………..
…………………….
on stage with my queen
        WRITING

[how cool hike whose?]

1
gang stir bring
the drama
ninja star
on the armor
for the former king
(like A Knight:
    stillshining)..

2
tomorrow i will be
A spirit steering free.
today i have to blaze

3
the roads & codes & odes
the debts owed
bets owed
the sweat soul & soil
ghetto********'s
star*******ving loyal

4
roachrat
throwback
dontclean
jack…

& now look
how dollars
look when
people look

for work
to survive
this rat
trap…

tracking dirt
on [WELCOME MATS]
cuz look what drugged
        the cat

5
i can/t stand back puff
cant standbak
can't stop won't stop
know that's that

6
city sap
syrup sweet
ghetto streets
cracked

7
at this point
guns point &
lunar
lungs collapse

8
how ugly
does it get
for this money?

ain't no
answer it's
uglier than
cancer gets
    at its
most Unanimous

9
find the time
to unwind
& just chill
out & let
the sun shine

10
that's all eye
had on my mind.
not much of A
mountain climbed.

[untitled bank teller]

making money makes me crumble
like paper in A sun-bull's eyelids
provided by pride in my iris
completely capable in this jungle of
Jumping Giants & Funky Virus
     i sit fixed & broken
eclipsed by my noble motives

& i wish U'd go get All that U can
     in the palms of your hands
   like the whole world in God's

depending on your Religion's Existence

& how long it's been
    on its Jobs of
JusticeGenocide
juxtaposed
just to show
(how nothing
can be justified)

bluffing because
this must've died with me
in Another life time in Another city
with Another mind-state with no one to pity

just A glorious morning sun
   shining brighter
   than any penny
      on me/
         belonging/
  to none/
               born babe/
          before bum

[Getting Over Dogmas]

it's tough U know…
like letting go of the ridicule
they hit U with in school…

like A General Principle ignored
        while U sit in
           the Principal's bar stool…

Beef-stewing,
proving there's always
something better to do…

losing, moving forward
with more words than
      U know to choose…

using
all there is
as far as resources
     can be used

& we
are gorgeous
gluttons &
counter clocks
punched in
& thru

[Water Break]

The camel got water
The cactus got water
The cash cow & mad cow
got your son & daughter.

This desert is dusty
The sand crystals lovely
& When I sweat I forget the
specifics I could've remembered
at A cooler more neutral temperature.

My sun is my pen.
I ink horizons.
I think my light skin
Might slide me right in.

My mirage is my god…
My job is my mirage…

U can probably find me
In God's garage playing
"GetOurs" Guitars.

[Beautiful Fool]

When U fooling yourself
and you know
you're fooling yourself
and you continue
to fool yourself
cuz you figure
to be
fooled by you
would be
easier to do than
by any one else
who just wants to
Abuse your Beautiful Fool
U may need to get sumhelp

[Beautiful Fool Too]

Because if they had A clue
They'd have A bad attitude:
& would BuzzSaw Adam's Apple Zoo
& Add that to Aladdin's Magic Shoes
& subtract what attracts us to
Theatrical as opposed to Magical
      & makes us grow irrational
In contrast with that which is Natural
        Or can be considered such
        considering this Modern Rush

[Women's Ears]

Whispering in A woman's ear
To push her til she's insincere
Will really clear the thickest air
     & keep commit-mints rare.

Because what they hear can be
                         persuasive
They often claim they've been
                         manipulated.

But today is the day of total triumph
     for any one hoping to buy us
Cheaper than what we are really worth.

Wishing to cause us
to pause our search

for work that works
     & play that plays

& women that listen & pay attention
But don't get caught in the blades.

[King Mean]

from his throne he's thrown
      jesters to lions
& treasures to Tigresses
whose stripes were both
      Religion & Science
which begs the question:
who is in possession of our idleness?

      & lies to us enough to
cause our laws to take pride in this
vice of A grip providing us just
      enough clean air &
   dirty currency in circulation
to survive in this Nervous Nation
   of nerve gas
      & word-blasts for
Old Kings
knowing
nothing
but

Over
Compensation

[He'll show you She's real]

did we not cultivAte
Originate & Copulate
from Atoms & Eves
All Nights & Days
& spin off of orbits all
      sides that sway?

or did we fall & fight
to stay Alive for A Love
      that lies in our face
blatantly as A Fire Escape?

to survive to say
we died with faith
In A better way
      than yesterday…

      What she says is:
"we should treasure
      our stay…
            Today"…

especially when she's pregnant
      with Another one on the way

[Quote UnQuote]

"The Juice of Truth
can only be squeezed
by A Wild Child Challenging!"

[long gone wrong song]

Trumpets struggle
to be Pied Pipers
Providing Pipe Dreams
within this Tight Hustle

& my muscle is my mind
& I exercise my love thru
        my thoughts

& what comes across
as wrong or false
singing songs as lost
as sound always found
with the people going down
by the river round the fire
    where killer bees
        & choir boys conspire
to sing the song til we're all tired of

    fighting God or boxing Blood
or knocking us up & out one by one

High
& buzzed
    Lighting Duds

[lovely ugly]

falsely bruised
falsely accused
I stand before U
an example of proof
that there is such a thing
as too much to undo

too much to unlearn
becuz even the sun burns
feeling its fuel fired up
& fierce & forced on
to our foreheads for years…

hot head aches & molten migraines
melding to help me find my way
to the source of the warmth

I seek to be heated & held
by mama earth taking care
of all our basics
    & complicateds

  Basically by her self

[Poets & Politics (double trouble talk)]

The powerful tower leans
Like flowers without their green
Strings strapped to capsules cap sized
In Blak skies of last cries & last breaths

Cascades
&
Caskets

As cash gets all the credit
And Money runs me without
Stretches of rest or sessions
Of warm up stretching
At best
I burn
And learn
Left from right
Better than wrong from right
Knowing every song I'll ever write
Will sound just like I was born tonite…
Fresher than the rest of your registers
& registries & refrigerated human beans

That bite
To Knight
Themselves
The Kings
Of What
This means
Tonight

[Typical Literal]

Type
Tape
And
Stick to
My faith
Like tissue
The
Issue
The Paper
The Major
pace of
The pistol
on its pedestal it sits like
A swollen load of lists too
long to read
the head it hurts
and the heart curses itself

For
War
For
Work
For
Whores
& Church…

& it hurts
to think this
much of earth

And air unaware
    How blessed
        How cursed

[thirst things thirst]

quenched by questions
answered by moisture
inspired by water
admired by daughter,
son & father: mother
of the under/over hunger
provides the harvest for
the hustler, the farmer,
the carpenter, the brother…
the hardest words ever uttered
the smartest words ever uttered
she is responsible for catching &
carrying them & pushing them out
of her mama's mouth:
& burying them with her songs
crying out like Lightning-Clouds
raining her pain like an Angry Child
that Can't Agree with this style of play—
this foul called this way—
this smile known to stone & fade…

this cursed thirst for things to change.

[say when (uncle bin)]

kitchen knuckles bend ants back
middle finger says DANCE—TAP…
& A whole bunch of hushed puppies
get crushed in my Hand's Trap…

rushed back to the theatre
to reenact thee act in their

mirror
ontopof
mirror
ontopof
mirror:

        A HELICOPTER APPEARS
with propellers made out of mirrors
& cameras made out of sand
for your eyes to catch like tans
in the parlor of darker than pans
frying chickens that ain't flyin' &
people that ain't apologizin'
for committing
any kind of crime
is permissible by the criminal…
the anti-subliminal fun-guy general…
the military we get to know
as civilians & children:

firecracker off the roof
of the darkest apartment buildin'…
to spark this heartless feelin'—to
light the darkness & start its healin'.

[trash talks]

my compost heap
can not compete
with my stinking
feat.

I am Stink-King;
keep
your mouth shut.

I am mouth
cut from
cow gut
& cow hide
& my cow
words
dye A
thousand times
& move like
kaleidoscopes
inside of eyes
dilated by dope
by the dime…
by the nickels in time.

in the nick of rhyme
got the knack for lines
to stand in line for bread,
for cheese,
for whine…

to complain of times
with no signs on
cards
bored with their
brilliant deal of
bomb-bards…

to scrap these shards
& unsheathe A heat
that is both straight &
hard & circular & sweet…

to convince the squares
they are to be smoked
like chiefs, like engines,
like butcher-shop meat…

    & Revenge sits at
the end of this street
smoking itself to sleep.

[All Purpose Tanka(s)]

*

days go by like knights (on horses)
flowers flush like toilet bowls
up against my soul
i find the dividing lines
on roads of metal petals

**

an introduction
goes without saying anything
to anyone at
any time it may all sound
like rhyme but not sound like mine

***

gamble soldiers &
roll your dice like bowling for
strikes in A bat-cave:
know your life is like ice-cream
& your death will be A heat-wave

****

thank you for the last
time I will have to say this
to you this way it's
basically up to you
to take it and make it true

*****

ants on knuckle points
discarded like a couple
joint roaches roaming
in kitchens like love-sofas
open for heart-shaped corners

******

does it matter if
it matters that all the leaves
are gathered like men
& women & children &
scattered the same way for them

[typing time (4)]

at Hallucination Hospital
i run too many units to be counted so
i throw pills like pop-bottles, like soda
& cider & fire & froze-up little soldiers—
pale-green as their outer shells fold up
like fliers, like pliers, like A cop inhaling A
doughnut…it's so cliché—the jokes up…
like rhymes & roller-coasters & up-chuck &
throw-up & same release of hormones…

the humble whore moans
what the pimp promotes
& the whore is not A her:
an imposter prostitute
              & purse & coat.

coat nails with jezebels
prize purse for faces swell
and none of us ever ate so well.

make cents out of bullets bent
into shapes shaped like shit
that come out counter-fit.

awe-mad
dam-awe:
ain't no
tellin'
what
that
man
saw…
in them
damn halls.

sequence/
continuity:
ingenious
scrutiny.

  Captain
Passion's
   Mutiny.

I'm done

[Braille Breath]

blame blindness for our lack of kindness
& cause cataracts & cancer throughout.
ashamed we can't see who we need to be
& can't open our eyes up with A new mouth.

we shut what we shut out & shut up & shut in
& shut down & shove on 'til the next one wins.

can you feel the signs of these times holding its lungs
hoping to pass out before it blacks out & never comes
back to attack the sun that attacked like world war one
two, three (to be continued by you, her, him, me—

       our enemy is here—
our any-me is: fear & lack of info—
not lack of kindness caused by blindness—
    if words were only that simple.

[rot bottom]

rock-ness
mon-stir
i've got
tuh
stop your
doctored
death bills
especially
the best pills
crushed
like a dust
bunny
jumping
up because
money
puts us All In
the wood-chipper
like A poker-bet
A roulette-red
& blak & green & gold zipper
ripping land from limb like
an ocean like a woman
acting off emotions
acting out emotions
while men crowd & cringe
& collaborate their egos &
singe like cigar-scarred souls
& repeat those same steps
toward the same death
with an extra eagle perched

[hard to beat]

beating off to beauty
he was A pervert
at the movies…
he was peewee her
man's mood swings:
paranoid & truly—
                        Goofy.

beating them off with baseball bats
she was blind as A cave-yard bat…
she couldn't escape the trap
of love in the shape of crap.

both were cartoons
cautious coyotes
runners of roads
A hundred pages
flipped fast in
one direction
then froze
in A time-capped soul.

they met under
raindrops
& sunset
& had A hunch
they'd be playing
rainbows & gold-pots
until the day they both dropped
dead
gorgeous
at the
flagpole
right next
to that
flawless
post
office
box.

the messages
they left
each other
meant A lot.

& it is hard to beat Love
when its heart never stops
beating like drums in the lungs
of the jungles, the ghettos,
the little building blocks
that we use as children
to build from bottom to future-top
to reveal our real loves like cream
              of the cruelest crop.

[summer buzzard]

circle rock rack crate/grate cut cat tongue...
overdose of open lungs & closed capped shuns...

A Double Album.
muscle in the cannon.
in this canon of conniving
like music in that cannon that is All
About Surviving...
                        Playing My
Strings

My Horns,
                My Ornaments
Arriving
like A Dormitory Freshman
conforming to their Blessin'
cuz it's the Normal Incessant
to perform like War's Weapons...
to be Educated & Mutilated &
Celebrated by Death & Elevated
                to depths & heights &
                    all the right questions...

school blues sweating the hottest reflections
like A magnifying glass on the ass
of an insect in the line of spear-mint
fresh experiments with death & this is life
as I know it now—A poet's style:
                        so i wrote it down.

I feel like A Big Gray Floating Cloud
Anticipating the brain-storms that will stoke
                My Smoking Smile.

What's Next
just as fresh?
I would like
to know that
    now.

Who's the best on this X-Press of
                trained thoughts &
           one track mouths?

& is the sun smart enough to
quiet down when it gets too loud
& screams steam into our ears like piles
of pancakes stacked back-to-back for miles
of butter smothered in syrup if it heard us
                      dried-up & drowned?

Or would it just circle slowly Around
until we all became freeze-flame fire-balls.
    Great Balls of Fire, *poetry & sound*.

[Hallucination Heart]

P
  C
 P
        L
      S
        D

Tripping on
Letters for
   Thee
Illiterate Loves

    We
  Squeeze
From our eyes to
  Believe we're
As blind as love

&
Need to be
To be loved.

[poetic-pathetic]

static-electric:
shocked unexpected.
blocked but connected
to all closed-doors accepted.

poetic-pathetic.

gasping & breathless.

masking my death-wish
by disguising my life-wish
while writing what i dream
to be meaning-full & priceless.

& if U are reading this
then (essentially/
unintentionally/
eventually)
U helped write this.

& i am
just A plagiarist
      playing
            with
          words.

[I'm Cool (R U?) {A STAR'S VIEW} N FULL ZOOM-n-BOOM]

Like A Martin Scorsese Baby
i am directed by my heart racing
[cinematography—stock-cars chasing
after the background cameras with the flash & the
safety (safely locked Away)
     i ride thru Amazon-Amazing
         High-Lights of My Life
in Blazing Jungles of Concrete Loves
you'd judge to be like NoseBleed SlidingBoards
    but i know just what i'm sliding toward
& so i search my soul again
for an open poem/for A Closure pinched
from its sleep/from its dreams
       where nobody bends or twists
         into images like this:
           thick film over its eyes—
only know-thing is to keep on rolling
with A multiplex of colors cut for another surprise
& each variable teaches terrible-terrific
from magical magicians that imprison pictures
to release them from their bids as civilized citizens
as the strangest strangers—syringe in the binge-arm of
              The Deadliest Dangers
but the Heaviest Hungers
        haunt my heart 'til i feel as Dangerous
as Thee Legitimate Anger of Thee Oppressed People Raging On
Hanging on to their HE-ROSE to be Liberated
      like A DOUBLE FEATURE (R-RATED)
[Quentin & Robert]: Grind House of My Mouth—
Oscar Nominated/Actor Exaggerated/Master Emancipated
            Faster than I can Say IT!

(Edit it Direct it
Cut it from its Nature
   & OverTake it)

[UpDated UpBeat]

not that Negative
ever said it better
than Positive but
it is obvious the
god we love doesn't
want the god(s) they
love to make us
fade our faith
out like A turn
table Kane &
Abled & Cradled
by the menacing mother
of our sinister civilization…

O thee Pure Power of Penetration
ReInvents Itself
Event Filled
Failed
Only By
Those
Lonely
Lies
Smoking like
Hot Hell
On Our Child
Chopping
Chopped Trail

Chasing
Nathan

[lonely only]

rhythm & blax & blooz &
shadows that move like
choreographed abortions
(*no wire hangers*) & huge
exaggerations abused by
the dearest & nearest to U
& whom it may come burn
with fuel neutral & new as
it burns like natural grass &
hot flashes in the pan of
peter & jesus in never never
land with forever ever sand
like Egypt, like Cairo, like
smoke signals for survival
like an unquotable english
bible built by cardboard-
carpenters & corner store
profit-errs without the shouts &
stirs that mock the word like
gossip-slurs & shopping-sprees
& cowboys kicked in thee ash
with their own spurs—A stone
urn for their private proper-tease
excited like they earned more air
&
this Quality Oxygen is not for me.

MAX/ON\ /MAX\OFF

Thee
O
Pressed

as Opposed to
thee M
pressed

I never noticed that
there was No Press
like Free Press
but what we've pressed
has us D-Pressed

& if every soul ever got
O
pressed

there'd be nothing
left to X-Press.

My bench-press inches away.
My permanent press temporarily fades.

But the pressure
Forever it stays like
mint-memories of limp lovers
during days of perfect loves
reinvented endless each daze

because to B pressed is to be touched
is like two lips pressed to celestial petals
& what we want is what we need
is how Love made us to be:—

Bravely Courageous
Escaping Slavery's
[constantly changing cages]

Aiming Anxious All-ways
Anticipating All of Us
Ultimately that

Brave & Free
& Dangerous!

typing time (1)

hunt-peck
helicopter
   sun-set.

the ink's wet
but can't keep up
with what i think
         yet.

in the image of imagination
i was shaped
& shot out like
chagrin & champagne
in the shape of imagination i grew
capes & wings & escaped from things
that were blatantly contrived to make me
         feel weak inside—
& though pain is weakness leaving
& though systems are instituted for deceiving
& even though people speak to keep repeating
i type to keep igniting
what I would've kept lighting
writing ripe reams of life-beams
inviting this world to wake in my day dream
tonight we
could be
on our way
to good tidings & fanatic-waves
waving horizons in like the plane-dude,
the plain dude with his mighty pen.

imagine
sand dunes
made of
paper castles
sky scraping
glass thru.

the end

Bubbles

soap-suds saliva spheres...
gang-blood & tribal tears...
snot-knows & snob-doors...
no knobs & snow-chores...

butterflies & cocoons
& caterpillars & hard-moons
& lather built up like high-noon
& the last bowl of cereal in my spoon.

fire-hoops & the yo-yo
vice-squad on patrol—roll
like dough-O's in the O-O
& it is nice to write on the stove.

burst first or crash last...
big burp or fast gas...
this earth is half ash...
the other half is glass...

no half & no whole
& no part to know.
like A quick shot of hip hop:
                can I get A HO?!?!
        to obviously reap
             what I sow.
    to not be obsolete—
            to be A memory/
            to teach my soul.

-MaxWell Shell-

to definitely
repetitively
freshen up
the tub &
love life as
well as death
consecutively
clean & scrub
& rub my role
into existence
thru sheets of
cosmic comets
concrete vomit
& non-peace profits
that set streets
up for the same
shit in A toilet bowl
to Excrete!
& Explode!

        & Astonish!

cabbage patch (over my eye)

1
They gave me babies
before they gave me
        A dull time
with dutiful dolls I
   did not recognize
with out crossed eyes
       and dotted tease
           eye shot
               it squeezed
                               me
out of its eye socket tree:

I
G I JOE
SNAKE
EYES

GUN
HO
I
SEE

2
to further explain
would be to make
Gerber of your Brain.

3
but since you
really wanna know!
just
cut thee Umbilical!
& we can talk soft…
                baby.

4
hey stranger with the fish-fin grin
wouldn't it be the coolest to do this
                    All Over again?
    —my friend?

5
card sharks & aardvarks
pool sharks & pool sharks
& new larks to lark with
to Market Depart Mints
& freshen the dead in
           their Marked Up
           Sweet Heartless

6(to the beat goes their target)
Aim,
am I stealing love like home-base?, yes…
Me—of all species—
above
all feces,
love, law & leases & leashes…
& renting this pen from A friend:
                          telekinesis.
priceless
super
features
for this future
of Holy Jesus
Holy Moses &
Holy Divas
holier than thou bleachers
cuz ain't nothin' but space
           between us

(holier than my high school bleachers
cuz ain't nothin' but pride-fooled/
           foolish space between us)

7
she learned early
she would burn & keep burning
she would burn & get burnt &
the world would keep turning
& she could keep learning
if she chose to keep earning
her turn & her time served like
           permanent crimes.

8
I have been
rehabilitated
& wasted in
the same line
as they've been
waiting on mine.

9
no longer for fun
never ever for fame
no long-err
of strong words
for pleasure or pain.

words like (an epic epilogue) kudos to who knows

Words like furniture
sitting in the living room
    living in the den
desperately desiring
    dusting off again.

Words like human-war
fighting over skin-tones
god's bones & thin-coins
collected when the pen joins.

Words like Fear-Joy:
A new mirror to M-ploy
with compound god-sounds
& dictionary's to destroy
in the background's kid-noise.

Words like water
that I say to your daughter
to offer her pureness
amidst this obscure kiss.

Words like fire
that light me on fire
that provide me the fire
I need to be fire on fire
double-flamed brain inspired.

Words like love
that draw blood
and cause blood
to paint & pulse
& show us who's boss.

Words like hate
that ain't that great
but U should see
how much love they take
(from you & me).

Word like cards
that get shuffled like stars
on constellation-tables
dealt like mercury, mars,
earth—first—yours—ours.

Words like blues
dedicated to muse
upon muse Amused
by the way they play
regulated by rouge.

Words like people
from liquid to solid
to baby to toddler
to puberty to future
      mother & father.

Words like prayer
wishing for warmth,
guidance, support,
kindness, reality
wrapped in this sport.

Words like kisses
capable of passing
the depths of souls
off the pedaled lips of A rose:
      Transcending/Entrancing.

Words like sex
excruciating extremes
to become one with one's dreams
and to wake in the same wet spot
that left hot marks on warm hearts with iScreams.

Words like faith
forced to act certain ways
forced out the mouths of slaves
A force reinforced for the freedom
      we've been promised per sé.

Words like Faith
     Taken & Given
In the Truest of Trust's Clutch
SuperNaturally SteppingUp to
     To set us up for UP…
        UP & AWAY:
SWEET TRUE COOL MIRACULOUS FAITH.

    Words like heaven
as beautiful as you could imagine
     with passion and unconditional
Love you could listen to all day/all ways
and never get tired or bored or cynical.

Words like work,
connotation: labor—
as in sweat, blood, tears
    worth every drip
    over these years
       less favored.

Words like Generation & Regeneration
calming any anxiety I may have had
worried about what the youth will do
when cut off from their mom & dad…
they will grow new family limbs
& plant new international flags.

They will be the words we use
when "the worst" is "the news"
as well as "the best times"
    we'd ever have.

about my future poetry

no more Happy Endings…
just Abandoned Burning Buildings.
no more Learning Children…
only Reality Television.
no more Romance Novels…
only if she swims & swallows
the salt from Lost Rivers that give us throttle
& torque & new news to report tomorrow…

                only if his heart is hollow
            will he allow this future to follow
the shadows that battle with age & sorrow
in various ways he buries his grays & borrows
        Day Light saved by his Myths & Morals
to pay for The Daze that knows no Quarrels…

& is quite content waiting for Night to Fight
to corner the pimps & the lights they light
           with match to mouth—
                            quickfast & Out!

he writes
he writes
whiplash & clouds
of smashed in
Avalanches
Aimed at Ashen Smiles.

Spontaneous Angles (for Guardian Angels)

if we believe god in the devil-sense
or in the god we trust perched
on the bax of ded prezidense/
                         we sell-dim
                         spend light
                         like we know
                                 we glow
           and can afford more
      than the price of gold
for tea & rice prices inside
      A Wild-Iris Rose drinking
titanic pints of Overpriced Love

     standing over A Costly Commode...

     reading Bukowski i now see my road
is longer thanks to Guardian Angel
                          Saving Angles

       & Odes
to All the Good Things
    & Bad Things We Owe
our little existence in this
physical-tense of signifi-cents to-
                       morrow
                    grows

                like A *Bone Palace Ballet*
                     out of
                 Pointed Toes

Haikus Too

*
Love lays like No One
Today knows the way to where
Love is in the Air.

**
Hate Precipitates
A thin-rain of complain and
can't-stand/kick-stand drained.

***
thin lines define fine.
thick books look like too much time.
i just want to rhyme.
have fun. have A feast.
have at least A little piece
of the bigger peace.

****
coughcough coughs the sick
doctors/lawyers politic
& I'm stuck with the same shift…

*****
moo kissed by the moon's
lips & the cow words in the
unlikely knight shining

******
last one: loaded guns
shot at students on the run.
tragic as they come.
(or)
tragic as they know would come
teachers teach & teachers run
the classrooms with bad grades
& pop-quizzes & Straight A's!…
A pokerface is needed for this evening's
pro-seedings—feeding our fear or our faith
either way we grow easy…we show these things

that do tempt us that we can really run with them
& we are fast & we can crash & we have every right
every rhythm/every ripe ammunition and we have the power
   to make Any & Everyone listen…
  once we get Any & Every One's Attention.

****
i lost my last thought.
i wish i had time machine
  to wipe my ash off

Words Ain't Massive Enough

what has happened
has occurred to A
mass that has heard
enough of the lectures
& sad gestures with words…
our weather has upset-stomach
our weapons have indigestion
our women keep having babies
which makes me beg the question:
who is winning in this one?
who is worthy of warmth?
    & who in this too-soon
      future is hurting more?
i have no answers for this one
other than feeling this sickness
      unknown to skin & bones
      that dwells within my spirit
& sighs A level of release &
relief to be at peace with those
that had to leave/had to go
like an Asiatic soul that glows
with shined-up-china grinding
crystal-pistols popping
bullet-proof vinyl-vest
maroon-five hat topping
singing this tragic cacophony
concocted by A Double-Entendre Monster
shining on all sides of our Hypocri-Sea—

horizons hiding thee common kamikaze in each
(it's just most don't act on what they think)
but there is hundredyear-frustration mounting
& A younger generation still counting
on its elders & peers to help them out & out we
                            go
with our dirty dirty loads of laundry to wash
        but i'm not talking 'bout clothes…
who knows what is unfair anymore—
any job—any time—any crime—any score
with referees that ignore the true penalties of life—

thee inconsistent ecstasy of price—what can be afforded—
what is allowed to be distorted—what's right?—all for A reason
when the Cliché King is on his way back
with his back to his King-dim with
words that sing them to sleep then
when they wake
they break even in the oddest ways—
while mirages of what God is get to work
        & play in mind after mined
                interpreted
            differently
                  days after daze—

but Evolution is not Human—
at least not
the Illusion we'd
like to believe
where we are evolving
& Thee Universe is still revolving
Around US—the sound of
Popularity & Polarity & Powdered Puffs
            of gunsmoke & younghope
                simultaneously crushed.

Words Ain't Massive Enough.

Free Verse for thee Uni Verse (one)

branches, as one, collect & connect as leaves
contrast & compliment with hues hung from
balcony-ceilings; windows with pillows for
eyes & sleep for breath & autumn for fall &
spring for summer & neither means more
to thee other than thee other
but Mother is from Another
panic.

swing low sweet charity
& bring me down with U…
these lips, on loan, that i'd
kiss you with, are not that
kind & gentle…considering
thee Origin of their Ghetto…
consider: with words we
hurt like hospitals & heal
like GOD's BIG initials…
both doses Overly Mental
without the mouth blowing
OM like A whistle…calm
i am—in this thistle
         down with you—
of course i'm A horse named Dribble
because i travel on thee backs of sunsets
and escape thru the cracks of concrete
because as LARGE as i am—
                i am that little.

that little light at the end of
tunnel-visions sent up wind-pipes
to risk Truth for Fame as fickle as
the names they'd forget you were called
before pointed fingers became broken branches
when windows fall to sleep with yawns bronzed
into winter wite-walls on dumptrucks with dumplings
dumped & leaning like soft eyes for sore-sight stuffed…
tufts of blizzard-news & closed schools & A whole globe
focused on teaching "The Fools"—whoever we are…
whoever we think we are—*we're cool*.

A short one for more won

i like to write—
can't U tell?...

i also type &
paper trail...

i luv lucille—
she's surreal...

she is simple,
makes me feel

like all could be
A book to read

to write/revise
      & improvise...

Firm Grip (A No Pen Poem)
...an open poem

1
Malleable Valuable…
Baby at its Baddest Pose—
no picture could catch visual inner-g yet
until they invented it—A 5th
dimensional set of lenses & lithium—A
6th sense of getting U to smile when the
sun sets—A sunrise kind of wakeup with
not another thought on my mind i make up
words as i go along to the sameoldsong
that plays in my head like A young
king kong before New York & Jane hit like
A plane-fist flying by Natives…
no no knee grows like the legs did…
i'm reading about Soul & Creole & Chicago Jazz—
Leroi is layin' lines down like lion crowns
for the kingdom to follow to find my way in
my keys are cleaner than alcohol & razors…
and straighter…and they say that A fool
& A child have favor & I am both until the day
i'm saved or baptized or prayed for A
thousand times A picture's worth—
what reflections of Heaven in River's church…
                    what ripple of riddle—
                    what middle, end, first?

2
What synonym
worse than
      dead?
is it done?
is it over?
did U hear what i said?
did U get where i was headed with the story
before beheaded was the punishment
                    they gave me
              instead of purgatory?

3
Words are Glory
as we give them it—
The Lion is Roaring!
(No Witnesses)
(No Special King Privileges)
thesamecliché…
(Know who U R dealing with)

4
balloon-bum pops his own gum.
donut-cop got a hole from his own gun.

they both stick to the streets like licorice in the heat
on the concrete on repeat—it's too easy to skip A beat
with your heart cuz you're smart & U know that—
so you're Arrogant & A pro at going so back
so far soul-blak//soul-star U R like so close but so far
in America's Home our place is replaceable with new babies
                                                        that know our
                    little-saint-nick-names
for the games we're playing
                & will play them
for A freedom ride—A cheaper high than just going crazy!

STAR STUDENT[s]

Celestial Cerebellums—Constant Constellations
    SuperStar Gazing Brains & Hearts
  in A Cosmos of Souls we are Brave & Smart!

We have survived crunch & much
& seen more than your Average Art on A wall
& what we call cool U might call cruel
                (but we ignite each fuse)!

We refuse to lose our lessons!
We are blessed as well as blessings!
We were born to per-fect perfections!
We are stars beyond any school's rules
                or paid profession!
We are Imagination's Greatest Weapon because
We can shoot down thee Unnecessary
& uplift
this gift
this present we're presented with
by recognizing thee infinite limitless
poetential in each…& just as quickly
as we can learn we can teach
& we do & we will until who knows when—

we'll just keep goin': Super Novas Explodin'
& Spreading/Expanding/Connecting like
close friends with Extended Family Members
          closed in!—but OPEN!

      O PENS & POTENT POEMS!!

O CHILDREN CHOSEN TO BE MORE THAN
EVERY THING EVER DREAMED BEFORE THEM!!

INDIGOLDEN CHILD

THEE
INDIGOLDEN
CHILD
    she's carrying now
    is going down in history
   as A Velvet-Violet Victory

   A Smelling Smiling Memory
with its senses as intense
    as Tennis Aces/backhands
      & baseline traces
   with invisible blue
     glowing over
       their faces.
They call it AURA
     TEMPORA
       O LORD OUR
          LANGUAGE
is telepathically taking us
   to wherever it needs to take us!

Transparent Air Transporting More Breath
      to breathe today It's
    Teleporting/Escorting
     OUR GREATEST
    offer for A PHENOM FUTURE
   Anticipated as if Greatness is granted
    but still can't be taken for granted...

NEON-COURAGEOUS
ROYAL-FOREST PLANET
LOYAL-CHORUS LANDED
      like all we know
     has been imagined
     up to this Thought's point>

         IMAGINE!

Her Age is no-matter
when her Inner-Gold's been Mastered
       when her Indigo
     lives after letting go of
      A glow that gathers
       like Soul-Soap
    cleaning dirty demeaning chapters
       not worth reading
         in search of
       deeper meaning
       see her screaming:

       RELEASING MASTERS!

The children that

died in Terribly Tragic
Holocausts Genocides
Pillages Massacres
Reappear to be here
As habit/tats that can
Be broken—A Re In Carnation
Of built up karma for
Self fulfilling majestic moments

Or, unfortunately
        & unfavorably
Focus can be placed on
Thee already Waging Wars
     & Excessive Explosions…

It is our choice to be

Indigolden & Chosen

Or drifting decisions
Frustrated & Explosive

When in the realist reality
We are capable of A Great Love
        that distracts
All hate & hopeless hope &
Mpacts like A soulfull Mplosion
that Generates Genuine Generous
     Juxtapositions Juxtaposin'

& sits Justice in A Gel Cell
     For cooling off
   not for proving wrong

& if U feel U belong to the
Child that Free Styles
& Brings Smiles
& Helps Out & Heals Now
& Builds Up & Breaks Down
The brilliance bestowed
    That we've owed to
Our selves & every One else
    For soul long

Then please dew what you dew

& may your grass grow greener
    & your flash glow cleaner
        & your past know an
Extreme Dreamer like me———>>

            Shooting the Future Free

The Children That Wondered Why

& contemplated how
To realize their world
Was an Impromptu FreeStyled.

& to concoct new styles
To move food to move bowels
Would prove worth thee effort
If fellow beauty fuels worked together.

"Hello Heaven" they would say
To anyone that passed their way.

"How can I be of satisfying service?",
Would be their LongLasting
      EverLaughing purpose.

Their Baby Nature
Instant Mimic Innovator
Appealed to Attractively
Would Be Great Even For Gravity.

Talk About an Up Side
                Down.

The children that wondered why
& contemplated how
Came up with the greatest creations
From Imagination's Soul-Down
U would swear they've
      been here before.

Like thee Ocean & Shore.
Like the sky & like clouds.

They'd gouge out the I's
Of Any Infamous Past
& blast it on silver screens
Hatched from disciplined
      Film & Scenes
To inspire us to never relapse &
         Go Back.

"Go Green
Grow Gray"
They'd say.

[No *ClockWorkOrange*
   GrowingStrong ToDay]

No Slogans.
Only slang
In the shapes of Love
On its way to heal
Whatever's still ill & plagued.

On its way to finish
What it started Any Way.

"A PO M"

Consistent-Sea is
The Key Note Speaker…

I am A sea-mint
        mix of Andy
  & Bob Kaufman,

        Lost in
A space-man on the
FunnyBone's Moon,

Seized by my city's spirit &
        Country's Poetential
        Within A wealthy world
        Worthy of Its Every Eventual…

The laughter the silence
        is AllWays Essential…

The Master is priceless
        (Within U):

                Continue

BIO BOW (OUT)

MaxWell Shell was Born
in Cleveland, OHIO
in A hospital now gone
but once known for
      Suicide Notes.

Having never met
his Irish side of the family
due to A diss-owning issue
involving his late great mother's love
      for his been-lost father;
he can't help but relish in his poetic
stellar rebellious that dwells within
his very starched & fired-up fibered being.

His writer life was initiated in on the
      darker side of things
   only to show him how
      much *DayLight* needs The **LateNight**.

His paler elders consider him A **BLAK.POET**.
His Peerless Contemporaries just think he's
Crazy BeautyFueled with an UnRivaled Love innerG.

He considers himself
an extremely dreamy
   IndiGolden Poet
steeped deepsea deep in
The Realest Realist RealiTea.

An Ideal Space to be.

   He feels blessed
to be chosen to X-press.
i.e. He continues to use
   his poetic license
to drive quill-legally
      outer space.

At times (most times)
U will see **black** & *white*
spelled BLAK & WITE to take
out the   Color
          & Hate.

    He's been doing this since
choosing to do so at the Age of eighteen.

        Word to his Mothers.

            (LOVE IS LUV)
  &
Typing
In third
    person
can be A great thing.

(MAX OUT)